D0269488

# Diwali

## Katie Daynes

Illustrated by David Dean

Designed by Karen Tomlins

Reading consultant: Alison Kelly
Roehampton University

Diwali consultant: Seeta Lakhani
Photographic manipulation: Keith Furnival
Series editor: Lesley Sims

# Internet links

You can find out more about Diwali
by going to the Usborne Quicklinks Website at
**www.usborne-quicklinks.com**
and typing in the keyword *Diwali*.

Please note that Usborne Publishing cannot be
responsible for any website other than its own.

## ACKNOWLEDGEMENTS

© **ALAMY** p1 (Vivek Sharma), p9 (Tim Gainy), p18 (UK Alan King);
© **CORBIS** front cover (Reuters), back cover (Bill Ross),
pp4-5 (Pawan Kumar/Reuters), pp6-7 (Ajay Verma/Reuters),
pp14-15 (Bob Krist), pp16-17 (Manjunath Kiran/epa);
© **GETTY IMAGES** pp12-13 (Narinder Nanu/AFP);
© **Saiful Khan** p48

# Contents

## Chapter 1

# Celebrations

Diwali celebrations begin on a dark, moonless night. Suddenly, little lights appear around the streets. Fireworks explode in the sky and excited voices fill the air.

Diwali is a festival where families and communities come together. They give thanks for the year that's gone and hope for a happy year to come.

A catherine wheel swirls sparks into the sky at the beginning of the Diwali celebrations in Lucknow, India.

Diwali takes place every year in October or November, just before the new moon appears. Followers of the Hindu and Sikh religions celebrate the festival, but anyone is welcome to join in.

Preparations begin weeks in advance. Stalls stock up with spicy sweets and decorations, and lights are strung across the streets. Millions of little clay lamps, known as *diyas*, are made and sold, so people can light up their homes.

In Chandigargh, India, a mother and daughter work together making trays of clay *diyas*.

On doorsteps everywhere, people arrange beautiful rangoli patterns, made out of dyed rice flour and lentils. The patterns represent the order and beauty of the universe. They are brightly decorated to reflect the joy at this time of year.

Traditionally, the patterns welcome Lakshmi, the Hindu goddess of wealth and success, into the house. But they also welcome family and friends.

When everything's ready, Diwali begins. It can last up to five days. For many Hindus, each day has its own name and traditions.

Rangoli patterns decorate the street side in an Indian village.

# A Hindu's Diwali diary

**Day one**

## Dhanteras

Welcome Lakshmi, the goddess of wealth and success, into the home.

Decorate the doorway, make little flour footprints around the house and leave the lights on to show Lakshmi the way.

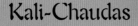

**Day two**

## Kali-Chaudas

Put on new clothes.

Light small lamps around the house and decorate the doorstep.

Some people fast on this day.

## Day three

# Diwali itself

Make sure the house is spotless. After sunset, say a special prayer to Lakshmi.

Keep all the lights lit. Go outside to watch the street procession and enjoy the fireworks.

## Day four

# New Year & Annakut

Greet friends and relatives.

Make new resolutions.

Cook delicious dishes and sweets.

## Day five

# Bhai-Bij

Celebrate the Hindu New Year.

Married sisters invite their brothers for meals.

Sikhs celebrate by lighting up their offices and homes. They say special prayers for the health and happiness of everyone on Earth.

In the city of Amritsar, Sikhs string lights around the Golden Temple – their main place of worship.

A Sikh woman lights candles opposite the Golden Temple in Amritsar, India.

On Diwali day itself, people meet up, give each other presents and share traditional Indian sweets. There's often music and dancing too.

Crowds gather to celebrate Diwali in the streets of Varanasi, India.

After dark, everyone goes outside to enjoy the excitement. Dazzling parades weave through the streets and the highlight of the evening is a spectacular firework display.

## Chapter 2

# Diwali stories

The word Diwali originally meant "row of clay lamps". For both Hindus and Sikhs, light in the darkness is a symbol of good conquering evil.

A Hindu woman lights a row of Diwali *diyas*.

Hindus light lamps to remember how their God appeared on Earth as Prince Rama and Lord Krishna, and defeated two evil demons.

Sikhs light lamps to celebrate the release of their teacher, Guru Hargobind, from prison.

The stories of Rama, Krishna and Hargobind are told in the following chapters.

A sculpture of the evil demon Ravana is burned to celebrate Rama's victory.

## Chapter 3

# Rama's story

Many years ago in India, there lived a wise old king called Dasharatha. King Dasharatha had three queens and four sons. He loved his eldest son, Rama, more than anyone else in the world.

Rama was gentle and strong, thoughtful and clever. The King wanted him to take over the throne. But Rama's stepmother, Kaikeyi, had other ideas.

"Long ago, I saved your life," she reminded the King, "and in return, you promised me two wishes. Well, I wish for my son, Bahrata, to be king... and for Rama to be banished to the forest for 14 years."

The King was heartbroken, but he had to keep his promise.

So Rama headed deep into the forest. His wife Sita and younger brother Lakshman went too. In a quiet clearing they built a small hut and lived there happily for many years.

One day, Sita looked out of the hut and saw a beautiful golden deer. "Oh Rama," she exclaimed. "Please bring it to me."

Rama took his bow and arrow and chased after the deer. When he didn't return, Sita sent Lakshman to find him.

Then a tired old man knocked at the door. Sita felt sorry for him and invited him inside. But the old man quickly transformed into Ravana, a terrifying, ten-headed Demon King. He had heard of Sita's beauty and wanted to kidnap her.

"You're coming with me," roared Ravana, and he whisked Sita away.

Jatayu, King of the Birds, flew to Sita's rescue, but Ravana sliced off the mighty bird's wings and he plummeted to the ground.

With his last breath, Jatayu called out to Rama. "Ravana has taken your wife," he croaked, "to his palace on the island of Lanka."

Rama and Lakshman set off at once. On the way they met Hanuman, the monkey prince.

"Prince Rama," said Hanuman, kneeling in respect. "Let me help."

He lifted Rama and Lakshman onto his shoulders and soared through the sky. On the horizon stood the island of Lanka.

"Ravana has an army of ten thousand demons," sighed Rama. "How can we ever defeat them?"

In reply, Hanuman whistled. There was a sudden rustling in the trees and thousands of monkeys appeared on the shore. They used stones from the forest to make a path across the ocean, then marched all the way to the island.

The demon army was waiting for them, clutching axes that glinted in the light. The monkeys attacked, throwing rocks and branches, and a fearsome battle began.

Rama rushed forward, firing flaming arrows. He leaped over dying demons, desperate to find his wife.

As he neared the palace, he saw the
Demon King.

Ravana turned to face Rama. "Your
beautiful wife is mine," he jeered.

"Never!" cried Rama. He drew his
sword and chopped off one of Ravana's
heads. The head grew back at once.
Rama sliced off another. But that grew
back too.

"You'll never see Sita again!" cackled the Demon King.

Trembling with rage, Rama took a magic arrow from his belt. This time he aimed at Ravana's heart. As the arrow pierced Ravana's skin he let out a long, deep moan and fell to the ground.

When the demons saw their king was dead, they ran for their lives.

Sita ran from the palace into her husband's arms. "Let's go to the forest," she said.

"No need!" announced Rama. "Our 14 years are over. We're going home."

By the time they reached their city, the streets were lined with cheering crowds. Each person had lit a little oil lamp to welcome them – and Rama and Sita were made king and queen.

## Chapter 4

# Krishna's story

For centuries, an evil demon had
been ruling over Heaven
and Earth. His name
was Narakasura.

Power had made Narakasura greedy.
He rode through villages kidnapping
women, until he had 16,000
imprisoned in his fortress. One day, he
even stole the earrings of Aditi, mother
of the gods.

"Narakasura has to be stopped!"
cried the gods. "Let's ask Lord Krishna
to help."

Lord Krishna lived in a magnificent
palace with his wife Sathyabhama.
He heard the gods' plea and agreed
to help.

"I'm coming too!" said his wife.

Krishna and Sathyabhama
flew to Narakasura's fortress on
a giant bird. They had to swoop
and dive and fight their way through a
massive army of demons and monsters.
  Suddenly Narakasura appeared
and released his secret weapon – a
thunderbolt. Krishna collapsed in a
heap, leaving his wife to fight alone.

"You're no match for me!" shouted Narakasura.

But he was wrong. Sathyabhama grabbed Krishna's bow and arrow, took careful aim and fired at the demon's heart. When Narakasura realized he was dying, he let out a final whisper: "Remember me. Celebrate my death with light."

Narakasura's evil reign was over
and all his prisoners were free.
   Krishna recovered and embraced his
wife. They flew home, arriving just as
dawn was breaking.

To this day, Hindus celebrate
Narakasura's death with lights.

# Chapter 5

# Hargobind's story

On June 19th 1595, a boy named
Hargobind was born in India, near
the town of Amritsar. When he was
only ten, his father was killed by the
Emperor's men, and he became Guru
Hargobind, the sixth teacher
of the Sikh faith.

Guru Hargobind wanted to avenge his father's death. He built up an army and wore two swords on his belt – one to fight the enemy, one to protect the innocent. He encouraged all Sikhs to fight with him for a fairer world.

The Indian Emperor at the time was afraid of losing power. He had already locked up 52 princes in a large stone fort because he didn't trust them. Now he arrested Guru Hargobind and sent him to the fort as well.

The Guru's followers were furious with the Emperor. "Why have you imprisoned our Guru?" they yelled.
The Emperor didn't answer.
"Release him now!" they cried.

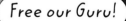

Free our Guru!

After a year of protests, the Emperor finally agreed to set Hargobind free.

Only if you let the others go too.

The Emperor thought for a while, but he didn't want to release all 52 princes. Finally he replied, "You can only take with you those who can hold onto your cloak."

So the Guru attached 52 tassles to
his cloak. He walked to freedom in
October 1619 – and the 52 princes
walked with him.

The Guru's people were delighted. They went straight to the Golden Temple, their holiest place of worship, and decorated it with glowing lights to welcome him home.

And this is why Sikhs celebrate with lights at the same time each year.

# Who's who

Here's a quick summary of the main people and characters in the story of Diwali.

A Hindu is someone who follows the Hindu religion, which began in India thousands of years ago. Hindus worship one God in many different ways.

Rama

Vishnu is the Hindu God in the form of the preserver and protector of the world. In the Ramayana, one of India's best known tales, he appears on Earth as a prince called **Rama**.

In another tale, Vishnu appears as Lord **Krishna**, who is married to **Sathyabhama**.

Krishna and Sathyabhama

Lakshmi is the Hindu
goddess of wealth, love
and beauty.

Lakshmi

Sita

In the Ramayana, Lakshmi
appears as Rama's wife, **Sita.**

**Ravana** and **Narakasura**
are evil demons, feared
by both men and gods.

Ravana and Narakasura

A Sikh is someone who believes in
one God and follows the teachings of
a series of leaders, known as Gurus.

Hargobind

Guru **Hargobind** was a
Guru who lived about
400 years ago.

# Recipes

People eat lots of delicious desserts and sweets at Diwali. Here are two recipes for you to try.

## Barfi

Ingredients:

1 tablespoon of butter
450 grams (1 lb) of powdered milk
170 ml (6 fluid oz) of evaporated milk
3 tablespoons of pistachio nuts, finely chopped
6 tablespoons of sugar
200 ml (6¾ fluid oz) of hot water

1. Melt the butter in a large saucepan.
2. Take the saucepan off the heat and stir in the powdered milk, evaporated milk and pistachio nuts.
3. Put the sugar in a bowl. Add the hot water and stir until the sugar has dissolved.
4. Add the sugar water to the milk mixture and stir well.
5. Pour the mixture onto a deep, greaseproof baking tray, spread evenly and leave to cool.
6. Put the baking tray in the refrigerator and leave overnight to solidify. Then cut it into rectangular bars.

# Pyasam

Ingredients:

400g (14 oz) of rice pudding from a can
2 tablespoons of flaked almonds
1 teaspoon of ground cardamom
a few strands of saffron

1. Warm the rice pudding over a low heat.

2. Add the almonds, cardamom and saffron.

3. Stir until the rice pudding is hot.

4. Pour into bowls and serve immediately.

Here's a selection of Diwali sweets. The
rectangular bar is called barfi, the rings
are jalebi, the round ball is ladoo and the
other two sweets are jambu.

# Index